The Fox and
the Goat

Retold and dramatised from the Aesop's fable
as a scripted play for three readers.

Ellie Hallett

This story works well as simultaneous reading for groups of three (Fox, Goat and Storyteller) as 'out loud' classroom reading.

The Fox and the Goat is also suitable as a stage performance.

How to get the most from this play

- The Storyteller lines need as much expression and excitement as possible.

- If you meet a new word, try to break it down and then say it again. If you have any problems, ask your teacher or a reading buddy.

- Don't be scared of unusual words. They will become your new best friends.
  (New words strengthen your general knowledge and enable you to become vocabulary-rich in your day-to-day life.)

Have fun!

Fox

I will play the role of the clever and shrewd Fox in this fable by Aesop.

I'm always hungry, so I'm on my way out to find something tasty to eat.

(licks lips and rubs tummy) Mmm – I'm really hungry!

Goat

I am the Goat in this famous story.

I have beautiful long and curly horns, and I consider myself to be very fit, extremely good-looking and very smart.

Storyteller

And I am the sparkly-eyed Storyteller who fills in the details of the action.

So let's sit down in a comfortable spot and find out what happens.

Fox

My plan for this afternoon is to follow the Buttercup Path to the river just before the sun goes down.

I saw a plump, fully-grown jack rabbit out that way yesterday, and I intend to have him for supper tonight.

Oh yes! There is nothing more delicious than a plump, fully-grown jack rabbit!

Goat

My life is very boring. I have to eat dry and dusty nettles and weeds all day, every day. Same old, same old!

Oh how I wish Farmer John would let me out just once so I could explore the soft green grass on the other side of this fence.

And what's more, a little bird told me

that the sweetest and juiciest buttercups and daisies are growing wild beside the path down near the river.

Just a minute! What's this? A hole in the fence. Here's my chance to escape! Ouch – not quite my size, but if I *(grunt and groan)* push hard, I'll get through. *(grunt and groan again)*

Ah **yes**! Success! Freedom at last. Buttercups and daisies, here I come!

Storyteller

Two things were now happening at the same time.

Fox was walking down Buttercup Path

to the river to find his plump jack rabbit for supper.

Meanwhile, Goat was trotting down the track from the other direction to find those juicy buttercups and daisies.

Fox suddenly noticed something he had never seen before.

Fox

Hello! What have we here!

Why, it's a high stone wall. It looks like an old well.

I'll stand up on it to get a better view to see if that juicy jack rabbit is hiding in the long grass.

Oh – oops – oh no! I've lost my balance! I'm falling off the stone wall and into the well! I'm going down! Help! Help! Oh bother!

Yikes! And I seem to be standing in water.

Irky perky … There's black slimy gooey stuff all over me, and I can't even see my beautiful brush tail.

Phew! And what an awful smell.

Yukkety yuk! Help!

Goat

Those lovely sweet juicy buttercups and daisies must be very near here by now.

Hang on a minute!

I can hear something. *(pause to listen)*

What **is** that dreadful noise?

It sounds like someone calling for help.

Who could it be, out here in the middle

of nowhere?

(listens again) Mmmm … How strange.

The voice seems to be coming from

under the ground.

Storyteller

The noise was indeed terrible, and the

ground echoed with the cries of Fox

calling out for help at the top of his

voice.

As we already know, Fox was at the bottom of the well, soaked to his skin in cold, slimy, black water.

He had tried scrambling up the sides of the well, but they were too slippery and steep.

So, he just swam around feeling miserable. Every now and again, he called out once more for help.

Fox

What a bad situation for me to be in! I'll have to think of a very crafty plan to get myself out of this mess. It will need to be a cunning plan, otherwise I could be here for hours – maybe days!

Goat

Hello! Is anyone there? Are you in trouble? Hello! Hello! Have you been calling for help?

Hello – hello?

Storyteller

Fox couldn't believe it. Someone or something was asking if he was in trouble! Yes – Fox certainly was in trouble, and he needed help **now**.

What Fox saw when he looked up was the most wonderful sight in the whole wide world.

To his amazement, Fox could see two big bright eyes and a pair of beautiful strong curly horns. Goat was peering down into the murky depths of the well.

It was at that very moment Fox thought of a devious and crafty plan.

Fox

(brief pause then spoken in a super-sweet voice) Yes, there *is* someone in this quiet and lovely spot.

I am having the most delightful time down here!

I was feeling hot and thirsty, so decided to enjoy an evening swim and at the same time partake of this cool, refreshing spring water.

I can see in the moonlight that you are a very strong and handsome animal, Mr Goat.

Why don't you join me so that we can enjoy this refreshment together!

Goat

What a kind offer, friendly Mr Fox! Come to think about it, I *am* quite thirsty. Fresh spring water is my favourite, so I am more than happy to join you.

(said to himself) There's something

about foxes that my mother, the Nanny Goat, told me when I was a little kid, but I didn't listen very well to what she said. I hope it wasn't important.

Storyteller

But what Goat's mother had told him when he was a kid **was** important.

He, like many kids, should have listened to his mother much more carefully!

But now let's return to the action and hear what happens next.

Fox

(said in a very syrupy voice) Oh, handsome Goat – this water is fresher

and sweeter than any I've ever tried.

Not even the nearby river water tastes quite as full of minerals and natural therapies as this water does.

I would love to have your company for some intelligent conversation, dear Mr Goat.

Why not join me?

The moon is starting to shine in here quite charmingly. While there's still some light, please accept my invitation to come on down.

Goat

So kind!

Thank you very much, kind Mr Fox. I will accept your offer. It certainly is a lovely night for a swim.

Ohh … It's a bit harder to clamber down than I thought – oh, ah.

I've made it! Quite slippery and a bit deeper than I imagined, but here I am.

(pause) I don't like mentioning it, but this water seems a bit, well, quite a bit less fresh than you gave me to believe, Mr Fox.

And what's that black stuff on your fur? Ahh – Fox – what are you doing? What is the matter? Where are you going?

(voice becoming higher and words said more quickly) Ow! You're hurting me with your sharp Foxy claws. Ouch! Now you're digging into my back with your spiky feet!

(voice gradually slows and gets softer) What about our intelligent conversation and a lovely drink of fresh water with minerals and natural therapies?

Storyteller

It was at this very moment that Goat remembered what his mother, the Nanny Goat, had told him when he was still a little kid.

She warned him to always look before leaping. She also told him not to talk to strangers, especially sweet-talking ones.

Fox

You're a real pal, you silly old goat!

(said with glee) Thank you so much for your generous help. Your small brain and big horns have helped me make my escape. Now it's your turn to have an evening swim. Goodbye, Goatie Boatie. Goodbye!

Ah, fresh air at last. *(said to himself)* Now, I'll just have a good shake and a roll on the ground to clean off that smelly slimy stuff, and I'm off!

(calling out loudly from a distance)
Goodbye Goat. I'm off to catch a tasty jack rabbit. (laughs heartily)

Goat

(pause) Oh bother and double bother. What have I done! I'm in really **big** trouble. Why on earth didn't I think before believing the words of Fox? And how it smells in here!

And I'm cold and it's dark. The moon has disappeared, and I think it's going to rain.

What if a storm comes? Maybe no-one

will come this way for months, and I'll get thinner and thinner.

Storyteller

Poor Goat. He thought of all the awful things that might happen to him while he stood there in the water of the dark well. However, Goat was also in luck.

It so happened that Farmer John decided to check all his fences early the next day. It didn't take him long to find the hole in the fence of Goat's paddock – and of course, no Goat.

After searching, Farmer John noticed some slimy black grass near the well, and he stopped to have a closer look.

While he was doing this, he heard the sad and plaintive bleats coming from inside the well. He knew that sound!

Fox

And now I will tell you what happened to me after I made my heroic escape from the well.

I hunted everywhere for that warm and juicy jack rabbit. Unfortunately, I think he must have heard all the goings-on at the well and made himself scarce. But for a crafty fox, there is, of course, always another day.

Goat

It took me days and days to recover from the bad experience I had in the well. Farmer John used his big tractor and some long ropes to winch me to safety.

It was not an elegant way to be rescued!

I have since realised that a diet of nettles and weeds has a lot more merit than I had previously thought.

And those fresh buttercups and daisies growing down by the river would have played havoc with my digestion.

I firmly believe that it's just as well (no

pun intended) that I didn't find them.

Storyteller

I'm not sure if this was the total truth from Goat, but I'll leave this for you to decide.

However, the main point of all this thinking and talking was that both Fox and Goat came to more or less the same conclusion, and that was to first of all …

Fox

Listen to your mother.

Goat

And, as Aesop's fable tells us …

All

Look before you leap!

The Readers' Theatre series by *Ellie Hallett*

These **Readers' Theatre** stories have a major advantage in that everyone has equal reading time. Best of all, they are theatrical, immediately engaging and entertaining. Ellie Hallett's unique play-in-rows format, developed and trialled with great success in her own classrooms, combines expressive oral reading, active listening, peer teaching, vocabulary building, visualisation, and best of all, enjoyment.

ISBN	Title	Author	Price	E-book Price	QTY
9781921016455	Goldilocks and The Three Bears	Hallett, Ellie	9.95	9.95	
9781925398045	Jack and the Beanstalk	Hallett, Ellie	9.95	9.95	
9781925398069	The Fox and the Goat	Hallett, Ellie	9.95	9.95	
9781925398076	The Gingerbread Man	Hallett, Ellie	9.95	9.95	
9781925398052	Little Red Riding Hood and the Five Senses	Hallett, Ellie	9.95	9.95	
9781925398083	The Town Mouse and the Country Mouse	Hallett, Ellie	9.95	9.95	
9781925398014	The Two Travellers	Hallett, Ellie	9.95	9.95	
9781925398007	The Enormous Turnip	Hallett, Ellie	9.95	9.95	
9781925398090	The Hare and the Tortoise	Hallett, Ellie	9.95	9.95	
9781925398106	The Wind and the Sun	Hallett, Ellie	9.95	9.95	
9781925398113	The Three Wishes	Hallett, Ellie	9.95	9.95	
9781921016554	The Man, the Boy and the Donkey	Hallett, Ellie	9.95	9.95	
9781925398120	The Fox and the Crow	Hallett, Ellie	9.95	9.95	
9781920824921	Who Will Bell the Cat?	Hallett, Ellie	9.95	9.95	
9781925398021	The Ugly Duckling	Hallett, Ellie	9.95	9.95	

KNOWLEDGE
BOOKS and SOFTWARE
PUBLISHING

www.kbs.com.au

Readers' Theatre